The Sky Inside Us

John Jenkins

The Sky Inside Us

Acknowledgements

Some poems in this collection were previously published in *Read On*; *Oz Burp*; *The Age-on-the-Page PDF Collection* (Nillumbik Shire, 2021); 2013 Newcastle Poetry Prize Anthology; *Overland*; *Mad Hatters Review* (USA website); *Salt*; *Wind Alphabets* (limited edition booklet); *The Drunken Tram: Six Young Melbourne Poets*; *Crosscurrents*; *Flagstones*; *The Great Auk*; and *Mok*.
'Ornamental Shadows' won Nillumbik Shire's 2021 Age-on-the-Page (Independence Category) Poetry Challenge.

Most poems in *The Sky Inside Us* are previously unpublished.

'He showed his love the stars
above the abattoirs.'
Rory O'Donahue

'All art aspires
to the condition of music.'
Walter Pater

The Sky Inside Us
ISBN 978 1 76109 237 4
Copyright © text John Jenkins 2022
Cover image: monstera from pexels

First published 2022 by
GINNINDERRA PRESS
PO Box 3461 Port Adelaide 5015
www.ginninderrapress.com.au

Contents

Dear Reader	7
Down Here	8
Her Decorative Weathervane	9
New Year's Morning	10
Looking Over, Looking Up	11
Midday, Nullarbor	12
Desert Waking	14
Sheer Delight, Tropic Seas	15
Heroic Sidebar	16
One Day at Circular Quay	17
'Pulsating Tourist Playground'	18
Brief Thai Photo Album	19
Fast Railway Cutting, Rock and Road	21
Can You Hear It?	24
A Space Apple Falling	26
The Rain Walkers	29
The Privileged Text	31
A Scotsman in Spondees (1)	32
The Daily Armchair	33
Under the Southern Crass	38
Shoe Biz: The 'Petrov Affair'	39
Notes of Distant Music	46
A Scotsman in Spondees (2)	47
Waiting Room, Public Hospital	48
The Pale-transparent Petals of Memory	49
Life: A Song Garden	50
Summer Poem	52
A Shower of Sparks	54
Diary of a Missing Poem	55
Breakwater, Evening	62

The Beach House	63
Seascape	65
Interior Waves, Words, Beach Walk	66
Autumn Drunk	68
The Seduction of Medusa	69
Into the Sun	71
A Scotsman in Spondees (3)	72
Tap Dance	73
Into the Literal	75
Dream Woman	78
A Quick Shake of Salt	79
Glass Paperweight	80
Homage to Kafka	81
Untitled	83
Atropos, to Her False Lover	84
Wishing Stone Angels	86
Their Oblique Inner Lives	87
Nine Riddles	93
Ornamental Shadows	96
Just a Dash	97
'Nature Loves River'	98
The Big Bang	100
Here, Sir, Fire, Eat!	101
A Shiver of Leaves	105
The Open Door	106
Notes on the Poems	108

Dear Reader

The silent interior tongues of words
speak in your mind,
                are a waking dream
and imaginary theatre
as your eyes flow down
                this page
and the next,
you focus on lines
        slipstreaming
                into new lives
and worlds of words,
only you, dear reader,
can now bring into being.

Down Here

Who knows the names of all those
legendary constellations, whose rays
no longer shape our days?

Instead, we stab at mobile phones,
step back briefly into life,
hardly glancing upwards.

Everything still revolves, resolves below,
as the Earth becomes an ever-smaller dot.

How many photons make a pixel glow?
How many stars in a universe?
Atoms in a full stop?

Equators turn tomorrows into yesterday,
and new hours into tomorrow,

all now streams
through time's dark window.

Her Decorative Weathervane

Her decorative weathervane
sits high above a garden shed.
In the beautiful days ahead,
see a sparkle on her weather vane.

Beside a roof of tiled sunshine
a little man rides his bicycle
in the wind up there,
it makes the spokes and pedals whirr.

No one knows where the first laughter comes from,
no one knows where it goes,
the breezy liquid laughter from her roof,
all we know is that flowers open in those
warm days after rain.

New Year's Morning

Pink at the edge of the sky, a new page
turns on rainbow holograms, disowning
night beyond the unseen river, where light
shatters a new calendar of days.

I make my blind go *whack!*
As curtains *hiss* aside
to a new blue sky where, everywhere,
hot air balloons are now uncorked
for dawn's champagne.

More rise slowly, appear exclamation marks
above a distant treeline
as their burners *whoosh* and coax
them further into fleeting clouds.

Their blue flames leap above a distant
vine-clad valley, a little further over
our not-so-new millennium's edge.

Then flocks of screeching, hobnailed parrots
land, slide down steep roofing iron
of our green cottage, still somehow
clinging to its verdant, unsold hillside.

Looking Over, Looking Up

Jim-Jim Falls, Northern Territory, Far Outback Australia

Your heart leaps, anticipating the shock of solid rock below,
blinks on this brink – a straight-down drop.

Below was once an inland sea, where two animated
dots now wave back up at you. Imagine a tiny splash
from here, drink it in, a sky-blue aching void, as timeless Kakadu
leaps 140 million years. Shout back, *hello!* down to
an ant-track valley's seam, as echoes chance a chasm's
sides, barely audible over a mighty waterfall re-bounding
sounds straight back at you, from halls of cliffs
and hard-domed escarpments. Today, tourists shout
against its busy uproar. But I'm still poised on endless time
and bliss, slowly slipping over, through an open door of space.

Drifts of misty cream, as more pebbles dribble down,
just a practice run. Everyone up here has cracked vertigo's
real secret: the fear – not so much of falling – but much deeper
wish to fall, to soar with arms outspread, from this rocky wall,
defying gravity, and miraculously survive. Like imagining
angels holding safety nets! This impossible feeling floats
you up and over, before adrenalin spikes you safely back.

The view is out to souvenir *you!* Climb down to earth again,
step by steady step: in careful slow-mo caution, join the dots.

Midday, Nullarbor

The desert is liquid glare
        and everywhere
        sands wander

We listen to dream winds answer

                as air scrawls eddying ghosts
                blue grains of sky

Grains drip in compact
        beneath eyes
            adhere
        to seal parched lips

Apparitions
like the horizon
            collapse to dunes

A high sun breathing zero
        semaphores lost days

Helical light
far and still as memory's smudge
            a skeletal lattice
against the grain of time

    Here, *now* subsides
like a feather of coolness along your arms

        This mirror sun
        so far beyond regret
carries your body
        upwards
            is sunlit
beyond time's fingerprint

tiny whorls pooled
    into honeyed light
        this world
        circling upwards
out of nowhere
out of legend.

Desert Waking

Sky-blue slippers   bloodstained hooks
whispers at dawn   monstrous books
filigree edges   their pages hushed
fables and tables   reeds bent at the flood
the secret intruder   canal and shadoof
music and magic   cats bask on the roof
sand-drifts of memory   trumpets of flesh
lazy carp circles   minaret suns
rose casement light   portals and domes
tears at the pool   courtyards of sleep
a distant blue ray   the wild dog will leap
music and laughter   daybreak like foam
a new princess yawns   dog brings something home
fragments of dreaming   libraries in flame
arrows and armies   war's shameful stain
moonlight on shards   a city of sand
bookmarks in the desert   her new story dawns
with a pale rose in her hand.

Sheer Delight, Tropic Seas

Beneath our boat
a long fish glides so swiftly –
spiked jaw like a spear thrust forward
through blue water

its tail hardly flicks
yet it hastes
        glistening through
our foam-flecked wake

you can almost feel it yourself
a happy rush
under waves of sunlight

almost feel that liquid light
slipstreaming its lightning
down your tucked-in limbs at speed –

and become that
dashing, shining silver body!

Heroic Sidebar

A tribute to leading Australian poet John Forbes (1950–1998) who died tragically of a heart attack, aged 47.

The dawn of a new era hums
with commerce. To keeps itself awake,
the cream bastes Australia's real estate.
Manicured in Hollywood, spearheading money's
pollen into gold bars, fake epaulettes
and reality just dumb daytime TV.
Is that a statue glowing or huge glass jaw in close-up?
Pity you're not still around to instruct
our toy lives, sort the tinsel chest of Americana.
Your style knocked awry the sleepy option:
poems with witty side-wipes rushing down
the rapids in some zany set piece.
Our foreign policy is still faxed in from Washington
(of course) leavened with brittle warm-up gags.
A stuffed eagle still hangs above that
roadhouse north of Alice. But there's enough
scholarly ack-ack in your called-in bets
to dine out for a year. The taxidermy
is free and hot-tub parties have run
out of fucking gas. Still, no clever anthologist
will ever leave you out in the snowstorm.
Now that's said, and off my chest, I feel bereft.
Alas, the bubble-wrap you ripped from base
parquet is all put back, a drone sings
Yankee Doodle. John, please come back
from your triumphant merry chairlift
on Parnassus, we need you more than ever!

One Day at Circular Quay

I found the true meaning of 'cool',
in the hip rather than Celsius
sense, while playing the fool,
      below deck
in a fresh white shirt, while caring
and not caring, stepping loose
on the ferry like a long-necked goose
playing zen friends with
the 'Generation of 68's'
      new denizens of poetry.

Fun stepping on and off
      a wash of waves
by the Quayside,
later scratching a pencil
on the sides of a cardboard cup,
      cheerfully
           broke
every rule and line
coffeed along to the wash and roll
      of waves,
with words
      I had just noted down
      played over and over
      like each new song's
own wave rolling
      along in the ferry's
aching wake.

'Pulsating Tourist Playground'

Formerly, an R and R playground for Vietnam war troops
on leave, this exotic Thai seaside town now advertised
in Australian tourist brochures, as *the* place to be, especially
for young males of a certain surfie 'tough-bloke' ilk. How many
pissed visitors have been led down alleys here at 4 a.m.,
left to bleed amidst its flyblown kitchen scraps? Pity, when
it really is so close to some truly stunning beaches.
The friendly kick-box spiv, or part-time fight-cock bouncer
on the door, returns and wipes his hands of all the empty hype;
the city still invites a mindless anaesthesia. In this seamy
nightclub strip, the police and crims both share a taste
for shiny suits. But much more for hard currency,
its doubtful economy. All this tawdry bling arose from the rot
of a discarded war. Here, domino stakes remain casino-high.

Everything goes gold-tooth here, for sale, including you.
Corruption served with every drink, in an endless carnivore
junket under fluoros; more sweet inane than you can handle,
barbed hooks both proffered and hidden, as crowds flatten
round a nightclub's glare in nightly carnivals of self-immolation.
The game here, whether slow-staked or mainlined, can be fatal.
You lean back to blacken a rose spotlight, as sad girls bat
and whirl, bars spiked with dreams like glad-wrap tomorrows.
Don't fuel this place. Never come back, not with a shirt still on
your back. See a doctor quick, check your passport and your
wallet. Read the small print, get out. Not another minute!

Brief Thai Photo Album

Video on plane...of my aeroplane flying.
Who needs to look out the window?
Fly 5,000 kilometres while sitting in your bedroom.

After endless movies, wake in stupor
near a stupa. Walk in temple gardens on day one.
If lightning strikes my *ushnisha*
(my cosmic aerial) then instant illumination!

City of Khorat, a train ride north-east of Bangkok.
Motorbikes, trucks mounted with loudspeakers,
for funeral ceremony, at 1 a.m.

Hoardings in temple grounds,
announce *Predator* video in café shop,
Arnold S. grinning, more violent movies.

Can Buddhism survive consumerism's
annihilating emptiness? Noise perhaps
depends on tranquillity as its opposite,
temple bells prompt introspection:
to see through this, what *wat*'s on the other side?

Street replete with traffic noise.
Japanese motorbikes and traffic snarl
plush radios, strip the skin, to raw noise,
new whine in old bottles.

TV resists sunshine in an open marketplace,
pop tunes on public address system
down otherwise quiet streets,
convey a new cultural other-worldliness.

In the old town are faded clues of traditional
village life, what might have been.

Next, piles of car tyres,
made into armchairs and thongs.
Waste not. Instead, cobble, reuse, improvise.

In broken English: 'This I very like.'

Road system not designed for huge
mess of traffic, becomes its own legal system
(noise, pollution, emission control
not covered in small print).

We become good tourists
(goods, tourists)
for hill tribes north of Chiang Mai.
Close to the border, at Mae Hong Son,

bright temple garden, bird calls, serenity
of welcome breeze in cascading leaves…
again, a universe converges here,
as with everywhere, always, forever, now.

Fast Railway Cutting, Rock and Road

glimpsed as the train
roars past
because so old
contains many stories
and, simultaneously, in the future
will always change

Stop and consider.
Only a few plants cling to this cutting,
many aeons since
our star's revolving satellites waited
for water, and life evolved
in billion-year-old seas,
all single-celled and simple
until a recent eye-blink.

In these seams,
heavier elements created
in ancient super novas
exploding out into space,
the gasses swirling,
where density of energy concretes,
forming solid bodies
like our sun, then planets coalesce or torn
from its endless debris.

sun flicker as train flies past
> its sheath of plasma
'promontories' of gas
falling back under the force
of gravity, releasing photons
on nature's speediest
eight-minute, 150-milometre
trip into my eyes now.

From the 'chromosphere'
into a densely glowing orange ball
fusing hydrogen and helium
in which some heavier elements
are still continuously created,
including carbon, essential for life.

Solar wind and flares,
escape of high-velocity particles
from the gravitational drag-back.

Before and after, always part of a larger cycle,
(ie, before *after* is after *before*)
> and this is now!

We look back into the deepest past
of light, in far space, as it arrives from
pinpoints and blurs of sparks overhead
in night skies, and into its future
> as it departs.

At the moment that you see it,
a milky glow, softly luminous
making today's day (re)appear.

Past and future interchangeable
in the one long continuum of time
always, present, this instant!

Can You Hear It?

Listening, listening…

It's funny how a whole room, a whole building,
can seem to be listening…

it's almost as if our listening
was also, uncannily, listening to itself
listening to the listening of others,
and to the listening, too, of silent things…

a small pool of silence gathers
          in one corner of the room,
as more silence streams down the walls,
expands, and runs across the floor

the whole room fills with silence

with a soft, still, invisible silence,
with a soft, and calm and tranquil silence,
the silence of silence itself

in this silence, you become aware of sounds which float
out of and back to,
and which move across,
and above and beneath…

Sounds of…	*your own breathing*
Sounds of…	*distant traffic and aircraft*
Sounds of…	*the constant hum of everything*

More sounds slip away
Sounds of…   *creaking furniture*
Sounds of…   *your own faint swallowing*
Sounds of…   *this white page you hold*

And, in between,
the silence which frames everything,
which frames the night and the day.

It begins to fill the room again

It begins to fill the spaces
between new sounds and voices.

Step by weightless step,
the silence is returning…

A Space Apple Falling

Imagine an apple, imagine its skin.
Smoke mingles with hazy colours
above the big city turning,
a world burning.

Through rich fog
over trees beyond traffic lights,
light breaks into a red haze,
bleeding into air.

Snapshots of the real,
falling into an abyss,
of random hits but mainly misses.

Staring into an empty bucket.
Hello down there!
Anyone listening?

It can never be filled,
it can never be emptied
like magical thinking.

So you imagine
an apple is falling in space,
its centre is red hot,
a dream of aeons,
as we also dream
it can never end,
as species come and go,
and more go now
than a very long times before.
An aphid-biped, on our apple skin,
with eight billion others,
whittling that apple down to its core.

That hot glowing core,
likely the origin of any image of hell.

I overhear a toddler
'flossing' in a supermarket:
stops, looks out and up, through glass entrance doors.
'Look, Mum, the sky…it's only air.
Mum, I could pull the clouds apart myself,
see, like cotton wool!'

As One Tree Hill
floats over the horizon
tourists streak overhead.

Another atlas shrinks
like a toy balloon on TV.

Such rare intelligence
resides in the human cerebellum,
reduced to knee-jerk self-immolation
by our more ancient limbic brain.

Inside the uncaged zoo,
monkeys chase tourists for lolly treats.
While ad men plot and thrive.

Then danger arrives faster than headlines:
Howling above the city,
and distant land-clear,
a new mine site, coal scar,
poison lake, factory, plagues,
endless profit growth until
nature slumps into total eco-death.

Silence howling everywhere!

Knock, knock who's there?
A threat too small to see
grows huge, everywhere!

Maybe one or two last chances:
care, mend, rethink, survive!

The Rain Walkers

Sleepwalking through the storm
the rain walkers
cup their hands with rain,
their eyes are clothed with bandaged clouds

Remember…
How they walk up and down night's keyboard,
a single white hand for the sound of rain…

The rain walkers drift forever here,
longing shadows,
walk down roads of glister and regret.

Their eyes weep eternally for all
that we have lost beneath the storms,
mere embers of the sun.

Faded shafts reach down to them,
sway rainbows on each bridge of air.

Almost asleep they read *The Book of Rain,*
the blurred scripts of desire

Remember…
walking up and down the keyboard,
a single white hand for the sound of rain…

Tonight you peer through cold windows,
you wipe away the mist, see rain glistening on a road
that leads to a distant river.
Your back now turned to the wind,
        you must follow them
down endless roads of longing.

Walk afloat with them,
        as the rain walkers
        brush past drenching leaves,
                in long robes of rain.

Follow these dark strangers
        where they gather,
             lifting long wooden ladders to the sky.

Higher you climb, to the highest rungs of storms,
where every careful step is cold,
climb ladders to an enormous drifting
                bruise of clouds,
        climb onwards there,
forever with the rain walkers.

Remember…
walking up and down the keyboard,
a single white hand for the sound of rain…

The Privileged Text

It felt warm, and cooed to itself,
born with a silver spoon in its mouth,
always served as Lit.'s most fancy fare,
sipped its own exclusive soup,
prescribed, cuddled and coddled
it preened and waved its wily wand
from every tute, syllabus and anthology.

But, as fashion's legions moved on,
was lost in new cruel scrambles –
pushed out the unit door, mocked then shafted
by a rabble of mandatory *kpi*s
before being fired from the canon.

        Poor once-trusty text!
        A rusty has-been
                left bereft.
Now waves from toppling bottles,
cold chip wrappers and plastic waste

        still wears last-year's wigs
        and old designer glasses
        in fashion's fickle dustbin.

A Scotsman in Spondees (1)

(Coach tour monologue, driving on, into these pages)

'Hello, everyone, this is your driver speaking. (Sorry, when I *tap-tap-tap* this microphone, it makes squeaky feedback.) My name is Robbie Doune, and I'm just a wee bit Scottish, dressed in my new spondees, and I hope you enjoy your trip. Or, as I like to say, *I-amb* Robbie Doune. Now, we are travelling at about two lines a minute, and will soon enter Prose Poem Freeway. Anyway, I'll be silent for a blink, as we pass this slow outfit, just a small caesura... *Zooom!* 'Yes, now, where was I? I hope you all have your seat belts on, which is required by law.

'Now, ladies and gentlemen, please settle back in your chairs and enjoy the view, as we will be touring through several quite long prose poems, all coming up in *The Sky Inside Us*. In between are shorter lyrics, where you can catch your breath. Our itinerary is various indeed. We will visit strange places, for those who enjoy the paradoxical, the philosophical and uncanny. Then swerve abruptly into silly side streets for readers who like humour. Plus many romantic landscapes, then several upside-down and inside-out, and frankly very odd poems, replete with riddles for lovers of language, where convoluted highways converge. Oh, and much more yet to see and enjoy. So refasten your seat belts and enjoy the next 12 pages, after which I will continue my tour monologue, ladies and gentlemen, and keep you informed.'

The Daily Armchair

Monday. A courageous young gunner trapped in his B17 aircraft follows a strange yellow light and crash-lands in a crocodile farm. Meanwhile, Hugo must come to terms with the homosexuality of his cycle partner, Max. Then Brenda and Ray step into the future though a portal concealed behind the NY stock exchange, where their dollars soon go into overdrive. Helen then learns the awful truth about her new art protégé, and must face him at the stolen Rembrandt auction. The action continues when a young 'torpedo' type persuades a gung-ho mercenary general to help him mine the yacht harbour of a ruthless drug sheik. And Robert is immobilised by a sonic stun gun that threatens to collapse his brain, as it opens hidden memories to a secret world. But can he deal with the truth? Then more amusement with tonight's Kitchen Sink Set as Elvin and the Chipmunks swap best sauerkraut recipes.

Tuesday. As lifeguard Eddie surveys the beach, a fire-eater on a bad batch of designer drugs spews a jet of flames, which razes his guard tower. Meanwhile, Jo makes no bones about it, she wants husband Mike dead for tattooing the name of his secret mistress on his arm. Corky, however, lonely for her novelist husband, flirts with a psychic weatherman, a flashy fast-talker with a ouija board aided by a mysterious spirit guide. Later, a nightclub performer picks up Brad who tells him about the private and professional lives of a group of high-flying Los Angeles attorneys. For tonight's supper, more zany Muppet characters play hit tunes on forks and spoons while cooking up bake-off hits.

Wednesday. An undersea missile installation is threatened by a carnivorous swimming crustacean the size of Hawaii, after 'Mr Diadem', a bizarre serial killer who preys exclusively on priests and nuns, leaves another black rosary in his latest victim's mouth. Ben panics when 'Consumer Sleuth' profiles him as the influential magazine's new 'bachelor of the month'. Meanwhile, a beefy gang mastermind unleashes the worst outbreak of crime the city has ever seen. Back in Forestville, Kate's intimate weekend with Bo is ruined by the arrival of an ex-plastic surgeon, now rock star, who fixed her face years before, while Bob seduces his scheming mistress in a new fun-park replica of the Taj Mahal. Then Q31 reveals himself as an alien, offering Captain Wishard more godlike powers, but only if he'll co-host a reality program in a parallel dimension. As a quick sneak snack, Donald Duck shows aspiring cooks how to ice more nifty cupcakes.

Thursday. A look at the dictators, politicians and presidents who have fooled entire nations, as contemporary art critics and game show hosts debate the issue. In the next studio, a diminutive Japanese tour guide and leggy dancer work LA's strip joints to infiltrate a diamond smuggling cartel. Max then acts! Making his long-contemplated move on Raquel, while Antonia languishes in the White House grounds, secretly watched by the President's 'play-dumb' media adviser. Later, Alex misses dinner but boosts his political profile by taking more bribes. When Doug's ego gets out of control, however, Paps takes drastic action, by impounding his new sports car as celebrities team up with reformed hookers and home viewer families to investigate sniffer dogs in training. In the backstory, things erupt when a hard-hitting LA columnist exposes a chicken farm racket, donning multiple disguises to solve a crooked banker's killing spree, while Denise confronts her backstage hysteria at the opera and Jay steals a kiss from Lou then takes a submarine to Lapland where he wins the part of Romeo in an open-air Eisteddfod. Plus the best of doughnut decorating and latest table tips from your White House favourites.

Friday. A trained dog choir barks the blues in an all-night fundraiser as a cop who blames himself for his partner's death is teamed with an invisible police woman, and they crash a weekly Wall Street finance wrap-up quiz, winning technie toys calculated to be the next big market buzz. Later things really hot up when 'the ghost in the invisible bikini' returns, now revealing her true colours, while the team delivers a stunning all-star hit-tune chorus of 'Balls in the Air'. If this weren't enough, things get really out of hand when Chuck Burnwild investigates the murder of several outer-city male prostitutes, before 'Mouldie Mudrake', the germ warfare specialist, returns with the portrait of a fallen Madonna: but is this a clue, or simple cue for more mayhem? Meanwhile, in a West Coast car park, UFOs unload the previously kidnapped editor of a bankrupt fashion magazine, just as Meave saves a kitten from drowning in her new bidet. This further incenses those legendary Creatures from Nightmare Bay, particularly after their fishing boat hauls a psychic dolphin aboard. It seems a mad scientist from another dimension, soon to be reincarnated, will now call the shots: but who will he be this time? Meanwhile, Geoffrey is exposed to a cure for everything, as the government tries in vain to recruit him to combat the outer-spacers. Then how to make eye-popping popcorn, as happy glove puppets butter up your midnight snack attack.

Saturday. A opera composer is seduced by a deaf mute servant girl, and they flee into the Vienna Woods, and there learn the ability to levitate after unlocking a magic gold chest buried for centuries beneath an ancient tower. Back home, Esme is upset by the discovery of nits in Julia's hair, live from The More Sparkles Shampoos Room, Los Vegas. While McCabe hunts down a vicious thug whose latest victim turns out to be Rex's old obedience trainer, Marilyn finds a new job in hosiery, but Ben's dream is turned topsy-turvy when a plane crashes through the roof of his new camper van. If this wasn't enough, Carol's baby is found in a bunker after her golf tournament ends with a disputed hole-in-one. To put things right, Erma conceals her private angst, even as a mysterious illness racks Kirsty, and Chrissie faces the spectre of addiction, while Jane relieves gnawing boredom with a new affair. But treachery and romance in overdrive lifts Gillian to new heights of resolve, as her trusted side-kick Doug dosses down to keep watch on Chief Lieutenant Speer, a cynical bent cop now secretly working as a 'con-sultant'. Doug vows to expose his former colleague, as sidekick Constable 'Red' Richard Herring unties a tangled knot of extortion, bribery, kidnapping, murder, disembowelment, and skipped fines. Then it's a never-ending ice cream dream, with Fat Ernie and Friends, as they serve more desserts to die for.

Sunday. It's pun-time fun-time again, when your Gee-Whizz Quiz Panellists ask you to identify clips from popular shows, ads and movies, and demand that constant query, *TV or not TV? That is the question.* Finally, by popular demand, the world's top three living dictators swap Russian, Korean and hotdog recipes. *Click!*

Under the Southern Crass

Night journey

Cobbled from land clearing,
        bushfires, smoke haze
                and dust-stained rain
our capital now fast asleep.

Tomorrow,
        finally lost in some
big slab-concrete tower's
        endless basement car park

Next day, another long night's
drive
        out of Canberra
past that roadside
        hard-rubbish mattress –
('free to a good home!')

        Lit up (again!)
by last year's
        old Christmas lights

but still popping out
        bent inner springs!

Shoe Biz: The 'Petrov Affair'

(A Cold War melodrama of 'The Menzies Era', 1950s Australia)

Scene One (Tug of War). In 1954, Evdokia Petrov is hustled from her house by thickset Russian embassy goons: no explanation, just frogmarched down the drive. Her embassy is 'displeased' after her husband, Vladimir Petrov, has just – *they* say – 'defected'. *Evdokia*: 'Comrades, but why? And why *me*?' Tight-lipped, they have orders. *'Comrades…???!!!!' Goons, in chorus*: 'Our enemies say Vlad has "defected". Enemies say is spy. We say, dirty lie! We say, Vladimir has been kidnapped – by them!' So one kidnap is countered by another, and Evdokia is bustled off to Mascot airport. She anticipates, after landing, back in Russia…what? 'Gulag! Long silence! One day, pistol shot?!'

Scene Two (The Airport). Crowds milling at the airport, outraged, whipped up by 'the news'. Enraged to save Evdokia, to protest, and drag her back…to 'freedom' (of the press perhaps). Jarkhov-meat-face and Karpinsky-square-head are her twin 'escorts', both clichés with feet. In Soviet-issue suits and hats – arm in arm, shove and hustle Evdokia up further, on to the waiting plane. Crowds surge forward, police cordons crashed, then dash to the Russian party! A journo runs along beside, shouting questions. Goons shout back… '*Nyet!*' But that press man's got the whole imbroglio caught on tape, and for the world. The crowd's collective hand tears at Evdokia's tailored jacket. The boarding steps wrenched back, furiously back. Then forward by the goons, back by the crowd again, as Evdokia's finally hoisted from the tarmac, up the steps again, assisted by the crew. In the melee

– what size, what style? – Aah! This fleeing Cinderella's lost her shoe! (It's photographed, and becomes an era's icon.)

Scene Three (The Rescue). Colonel Charles (Spry by name, and by nature), Director-General of ASIO, radios the captain of her Qantas Constellation. In Spry's spritely voice, there's no consternation. Her plane must refuel at Darwin. '*Must*, old boy. You see, so we've already got them! Ha! Tell Mrs Petrov, please. She can seek asylum in Australia. Be a good chap, pass that on. And thanks.' Meanwhile, Joyce Bull, stout BOAC hostess, kindly lends Evdokia (who's quite beside herself) one of her own shoes. As Ev slips it on her foot, hear her frightened, whispered voice: 'My…*guards*. They have…*guns*.' Promptly seized later by Spry's men, on the plane's necessary refuelling at Darwin, as is Evdokia herself, when the aircraft lands – and Mrs Petrov and her 'escorts' are reluctantly 'disembarked'.

Scene Four (The Offer). 'Now, what do you say, Mrs Petrov?' puts chief spy Spry. 'Good madam, be reasonable, just think carefully. *Here's choice one*. You can take asylum, live here with Vlad. start a new life in Australia, the farm you've always wanted, and melt back into quiet anonymity.' He winks. 'Or…*choice two*, you could…go back to Russia with these chaps, but to what? To Moscow, you're just a couple of cracked ciphers, of found-out, totally inept spies. And if you choose to go alone, you're just a traitor's wife…! And traitor to *him* too!' But her fears! Evdokia's family in Russia! Spry leans back, gives her plenty of time, lights up cigars. She's torn between the horns of…! Says, finally, '*Da…da! Yes!*'

Scene Five (A Political Free Kick). '*Yes!*'…says Menzies. A rare political gift, a glorious free kick, has fallen into his hands… '*The shoe*' emblazoned, seared into political folklore, on the very eve of the 1954 Fed elections! Menzies can't believe his luck (or can he?) The timing is perfect, almost *scripted.* He announces (no, he trumpets!) the defection: 'Commo spy rings everywhere, all our institutions are at peril, and a jolly fine Royal Commission to flush them from the woodwork of the nation…!' *A right shoe*, etched in the glare of flashbulbs; heel and toe on the tarmac of the public mind, the clatter, shock and heel-down etched forever in a nation's psyche. '*The Hollywood touch,*' mocks Labor's Eddie Ward.

Scene Six (We Pause, To Set the Scene). Three years before, in 1951, Australia (New Zealand) and the USA signed a formal treaty we called ANZUS. (The US will protect us forever, or perhaps drag the whole Pacific into needless wars).) To shore this up…*Menzies*: 'The fifth column, which by strike and sabotage conducts its own Cold War…' will be frozen out, as Menzies passes the Communist Party Dissolution Bill. He will lop the venomous heads of our Red Medusa! Fair sailing! But Menzies' CPD Bill is scuttled in the High Court. Unfree speech is not, it seems, a shoe-in. So Sir Bob holds a referendum next, in 1951.

Scene Seven (Evatt's Demise). Persuasive, with aplomb; Menzies puts the '*Yes*' case, the '*No*' articulated best by Herbert Vere Evatt, nicknamed 'Doc Evatt'; who, having tipped his hat at Chifley's coffin that same year, is now leader of the Labor Opposition (after a brilliant innings as first

President of the General Assembly of the UN). The crucial plebiscite is only narrowly defeated. (Evatt, take a bow!) Doc Evatt's sole victory in the whole affair. (An historic one!) The Petrovs were obscure at this time: Vladimir, at the embassy in Canberra, posing as a diplomat, really a lieutenant-colonel spy; and *Captain* Evdokia, his soon-shoeless wife, both with surveillance on their minds. Evdokia, née minor official of forced labour camps; Vlad, a false state's witness in lurid Moscow show trials; the sort that betrayed their friends for Uncle Joe, then wept; both hardly cleanskins. But, as spies, both totally *inept*.

Scene Eight (From the Sydney Symphony Orchestra (SSO) to ASIO). Posted Down Under, Vlad starts his so-called 'spying' mission by frequenting the strip joints of Kings Cross. His masters frown. 'Decadent gawping not surveillance!' But Vlad devotes his eyes to chorus lines. *Via shortwave radio, straight from Moscow*: 'Crackle, crackle, the snow this spring is thin in Vladivostok.' Code for…'Send hard info, Vlad, or else!' Because things are hotting up, it seems, in some sort of classified way, within ANZUS. And the Kremlin now wants answers, not some Bumbling Boris ogling topless dancers.

Scene Nine (The Mysterious Impresario). So enter, at this point, a most remarkable character, Dr Michael Bialoguski, code-named 'Diabolo' by ASIO, a mysterious medico and musician, and odd unlikely stereotype: 'Diabolo' casts spells with his violin, sports goatee, has hypnotic eyes, and musical skill enough to solo with Sir Eugene Goossens and the SSO. 'Diabolo' also moonlights for ASIO, and so now befriends the friendless, isolated Petrov... *Petrov (sulking)* sings, 'I'm just a Lonely Comrade Spy, a disaffected kinda guy,' he lets slip one night in his cups, at Sydney's Russian Social Club, where Diabolo plays on Vlad's strained strings. Which eventually snap. With this encore finale – Vlad defects!

Scene Ten ('Cabin Candidate'). 'Cabin candidate', in 1950s Oz, is ASIO code for 'defector'. Now Petrov is one, with 5,000 new reasons to jump the boat – in newly minted pound notes! ASIO haggles over certain papers Petrov must now swap for this cash in hand: papers penned by Aussie journo 'Red Rupert' Lockwood, mostly already in free circulation. But, much to the delight of Menzies, page 35 names three of Doc Evatt's own staffers as cherry-hued drips, as potential sympathetics, as leaky faucets. Menzies paints Doc Evatt a lurid red, and the Opposition pink. It's a parliamentary broadside, and Labor sinks!

Scene Eleven (Get Smart, Doc!).
Poor Doc Evatt, you have to pity him, no real head for shady politics, outpaced at every turn by Menzies. Rather than puff with outrage – 'It is despicable that Moscow should squirrel these spies into our midst!' (the smart option) – instead of gloriously fuming, Evatt declares the whole thing a farce devised by Menzies, ASIO spooks, and the Catholic anti-Commo front inside the Labor Party! All to secure a Menzies win in the '54 elections. Doc thunders, 'Forgeries sent to damage me!' Paranoia rules and he's lost his once-cool head. He blasts the Royal Commission, so it withdraws his leave to speak at all. Doc's panic deepens. He stresses

Menzies' 'Melodramatic and coldly calculated announcement to the House.' Deplores these 'Rabbits from a hat!' He stupidly writes to old-school Soviet diplomat, Vyacheslav Molotov, whose response is comical: 'Oh no, we Russians *have no* spies!' At a time when every embassy was awash with them, worldwide. Then Doc goes positively Sherlock over handwriting and staple marks, saying parts were added later, et cetera, et cetera, which just feeds the press and swells the general mayhem. Wrong move, Doc. You lose!

Scene Twelve ('The Split'). The Labor Right says Doc is defending the Reds. There are meetings, fist fights…wild name calling, all the way to the centre of his caucus, where Evatt blames sly Jesuitical conniving of the Catholic Groupers, pushing preferment of candidates into a wedge of stern anti-Communist combatants, the so-called 'Movement', led by intellectual Cold Warrior, B.A. Santamaria, Pope of all the plots against him, or so Evatt thinks. Splits widen. Bushes are beaten, reds found everywhere, hiding under beds. A special conference, with the Groupers locked out, who then form the (anti-Communist) DLP, a party that will fillet the Labor vote thereafter, all the way down to Whitlam, passing preferences in buckets to Menzies and his heirs. Menzies, now in Labor eyes a twirling Oilcan Harry (evil off-stage laugh, *Ha ha ha!*), adroitly calls a special double-house dissolution poll for 1955! And it's a landslide! Predictably! Doc's soundly routed! And Menzies romps home for the next eleven years. Meanwhile, Labor's 'Cocky' Calwell, one wing chewed off, just flies in circles, now left in an awkward flap. Menzies has it all tied up! On stage, now called 'politics', in his Lurex suit and high top hat, he's so happy kicking cans: *'Oo, oo, oo, what a little shoe can do!'* The Petrov Show, a flashlit icon of spectacular public theatre, with its endless tabloid twists: the lace, the double bow, and final slippery slipknot. Now Oz politics is just shoe biz!

'Shoe Biz' recounts the Petrov Affair, an infamous Cold War spy drama that captured headlines and shook Australian politics in 1954.

Notes of Distant Music

(Heard late at night)

Like photographs of moments
as they enter moonlight

notes present themselves
from her tiny hillside cottage,

seem nearby, yet distantly
flying into air,

notes are moments
never exactly the same

passing through
their *now* of new arrival

each pulse of being
a heartbeat
so brief

now aches
and tremble

as she sweeps her bow
across her true instrument of shadows.

A Scotsman in Spondees (2)

(Our coach tour monologue continues, further into these pages)

'Hi, it's Robbie Doune again! As you know, we left the Depot
12 pages ago in *The Sky Inside Us*, and now you can observe –
just by the roadside here – a rather spectacular hedge of
similes, all gloriously in bloom, looking as nice as…well, you
supply the comparison. But they always make me think of
roses. Again, now please look to the right, quickly, now!
'As we take this corner, did you see it, you did? Good! That
was Lake Dactyl in the distance, at the foot of Epigraph Hill.
A metrical foot, of course! Please have your smartphones and
cameras ready for our first stop, where you will also find a
comfort station, and can…' (*Squeak, tap-tap-tap!*) '…can
top-tip-top-top up, your water bottles, et cetera. (Hope you
didn't mind that surprise rhythmic burst, ha ha!)
'Anyway, there's easy parking on this suitably prosaic lane we
are now entering, so please put on your trochees and grab a
couplet of sandwiches, or burgers, at the kiosk just over there,
next to the chalet!
'There's a metaphorical signpost over it, showing a huge sense
of satisfaction pounded into the shape of a huge sizzling ham,
which – as I'm vegetarian – never appeals to me. But I'll leave
that up to you.
'I hope you have enjoyed the journey so far, particularly
through those wide-view prose poems, sometimes chugging
straight uphill. But the shorter ones, inserted in between,
provided a nice catch-up break, as I'm sure you'll agree. There
are many more ahead, until we reach the last page of *The Sky
Inside Us*. So refasten your seat belts, and off we go!
'Oh yes, I will check in with you again on Page 72.
Meanwhile, yes again, it's off we go!'

Waiting Room, Public Hospital

'Next!' The nurse taps her clipboard. *'Smith, next, please!'*
Smith blinks, and gapes, rising slowly. *Me. Smith?* Points to
himself. Still can't believe it. *Smith. Yes, I am.* The nurse is the
patient one now, as Smith shuffles to another waiting room.
Serum bottles wobble past lines of 'clients'.
Orderlies wheel steel trolleys in, the ambulance crews still
have much to do before their shift is shifted… Better just to
stare the paint right off the wall, read posters on flat feet, the
correct insertion of an enema. *'Huh? What? Are you still
awake? Still waiting?'*
A stretcher crew arrives and removes a body expiring in a
chair. It clasps a well-read magazine. A yawn voids into the
antiseptic sunlight, going pale…*going…going…* A minute
hand advances, *very slowly*, as Smith waves new bandages
above Admissions. *Gone!* But Smith must wait his turn.
Smith? I'm next?! Yes. Miraculously he stands, lip trembling
and staggers down the polished floor. The whole waiting
room must hold its breath; it goes very quiet, as if a miracle
had just occurred. His reflections ripple across the corridor
and fade where (it's whispered) an emergency cot is kept.
Later, he's wheeled back out, *and into legend!*
Mr Smith *is actually lying on it!* He's made it! A champagne
bucket is tucked into his elbow, hand stiff around a thin glass
stem, his smile the happiest of rictuses. Smith's a winner and
a grinner! The nurse fluffs up his pillows: *'Yesss…! Gooooood,
Mr Smith! The doctor will see you now.'*
At midnight, fresh from theatre, Smith trails bandages, wires,
a triple bypass… Then a blowfly, which doesn't have to wait
or wear white gloves, dies quickly on a fly-sprayed wall.
Lucky little devil!

The Pale-transparent Petals of Memory

fall one by one
in a shadowy garden
        of the declining sun
where red-faced farm girls
        leave their eyes on the grass
to watch for the coming of winter.

and peace is a little mirror flashing
when the wanderer smiles –
that we should become careless
after the harvest has been gathered
and sing fooling songs
on holiday evenings.

Life: A Song Garden

Alludes very briefly to the work of several writers, including Oscar Wilde, Arthur Rimbaud and J.G. Ballard.

It was an ordinary, familiar garden at first, which no one ever looked at closely, yet could become marvellous at first glance. A poem itself may also be a garden, of words and sighs, one viewed through your eyes, with sunshine and rain falling onto the page, again and again, breathing songs heard silently though your eyes.

Many years before, no one knows quite when, the soil was made loose and seeds planted amidst ancient stones, with new loam spread for bulbs, cuttings, small wisps of growth. To nurture and water was all, from the lawn fringes to garden wall, and then began a long wait to harvest.

Such individual and marvellous plants appeared, lending their art to air and sky. All around, they created new sounds, music written with the aid of flurrying leaves, music in and on high branches, fine rind of the wind, on every blossom, bud and stem.

Here plants of every description grew, in their order and section of the garden: cactus, lush flowers, and fresh trees, all with seeds, pods, fruit… The various beds were apt to songs beautifully sung in turn as ants hurried in weaving lines, each plant's flower gave up new scents, from their rare blooms, dancing with a dreamy light. Amidst smoke, mist, raindrops, there appeared cascades of warmth you could touch and feel, from sunrise to moonlit evening.

Minds also flowered here, in beds of pure memory, beds of wishes, rushes of wishes, and corners of story telling beyond them, with plots of vegetables, thick succulents in their humble beds, then rarities in rock gardens, where glimpses of sunlight lingered later as elongating, semi-transparent rays. Laughter soon sounded, as humour bloomed down garden paths, and songs from beyond the canopies of larger trees were full of birds, bejewelled beetles, as worms turned the hard soil over. Then centipedes, lizards, butterflies, moths and bees appeared, secretive small animals which, like filigrees of pure chance, all darted or briefly hovered.

In quieter corners were stone gardens, fronds, goblets, thimbles full of dew, stems both transparent and opaque, beads and diamond facets, liquid pearls in bowers edged by enlivening melodies, and sapphire and opalescent jewels where glades and patches thrived.

Here, roam at will to see Wilde Flowers, the Ballard-donna, or that Rainbow Lake (that rises up) and there the Burnett Rose. Here is also 'Love-in-idleness', a rare bloom that secretes a true nectar which, when applied to eyelids, awakens you, budding into sparkling flowers that convey wishes, or transport one to other realms, both when those eyes are opened, closed, yet open again.

A starlit night bloomed beyond these branches, where morning mist and fog sometimes shrouded or gathered, then lingered in bursts or glimpses. Bright day, then evening shimmered and murmured, all illuminated by a fleeting sun. Next, see fruit trees bloom, ornamental mirrors humming, sun-dials and garden statues that turn and salute your gaze, or seem to briefly shimmer in evening haze. Here all eyes become sphinx-like, when everything fades quietly into song now, seen and heard beyond the sky, if only you look closer.

Summer Poem

this instant
        your smile –
flashing!
a recognition of our secret understandings
in the corners of your eyes.
an expression passing.   now gone.
and my lazy acceptance –
        really a warm tide   ebbing
              back into awareness.
        with
concentration dissolving
into the overlaid rhythms of this day:

houses, sunlight, clouds of summer
dust swirling in faint eddies
              by the roadside,
a sap-filled eucalyptus
in sudden close-up pictures:

like this small leaf I see
        spinning slowly in the wind /
moving / somehow gigantically
in the huge surrounding space.
…slowly fading as concentration
              returns
back to delicate
              and merging flesh shades
the rounded planes and angles of your face…

elements that might go unnoticed
that I would like to fix
                so they sing clearly.

        each cell's division a testament
        to summers
        spent flaring into quicksilver
        of nerve and blood –

together
this day and season –
sunlight over
earth-fields of sweating vines –

transparent filaments
                warm with life –

this sun, flaming joy, soft flesh and heartbeat.

        reality experienced.
                tremendous answer.

A Shower of Sparks

seven short poems

Life
like instant coffee.
Just add water!

Lake Mulwala, Winter
Sunken bone-white trees
branch above and below
huge floating mirrors.

Conversation with a farmer
'Last year's drought!
Like farming pie crust!'

In any average life…
around six years of dreaming.
Imagine them end to end…
On a very loooooong bed!

Overheard in restaurant
'Generally, I think sex
should bring people together!'

Ego
ant ant ant ant ant ant ant ant ant ant ant ant
ant ant import-ANT ant ant ant ant ant ant

Dada cicadas
Thrum thrum thrum
Murth murth murth…!

Diary of a Missing Poem

I went on holiday, without looking back – bored with all the usual personae in my style wardrobe, whether excessively studious villanelle, languid love poem or sestina with bow tie and pretensions. I simply erased every trace of myself, leaving my entry in the new anthology completely blank, not a colon of myself behind, without trace. I slipped off the page, out of the book, and sighed…folded myself up into a deliberately prosaic suitcase, then carried myself carefully out the door, where the rush of fresh evening air was amazing.

Now dust kicks up from rumbling trucks, which loom and swerve but seldom stop. At the highway hilltop, with the sun in my face, I am now 'the poem nonchalant', 'the poem footloose', perhaps early Snyder or Corso, a beat poem of the open road. Thumbing down this stanza, I hitchhike with a stick over my shoulder, tied with a rag bandana, my swagman's pack, & jiggling inside it, against my back, is my toothbrush, a few 'cats', 'cools', 'mans' and ampersands, all set to a breezy bebop soundtrack. Ahead, I hope, is coffee, more cosmic truck stops with blazing lights!

I have been loitering here, in this mall all morning, with my hoodie turned down, and frowning significantly at myself in the shopfront mirrors, contemplating a smash and grab. But here's a better prospect: jump into some kid's flashy smart phone instead, and download myself as an app, to plumb and mine the cultural bedrock, from highbrow to lowbrow to no brow – in a flash of speed and blips, composing electronic get well and birthday cards on the Web, the thrill of slumming it, through a million avatars and icons, recoded into html: the icing on a delicious frothy shlock, digital delinquency. *Watch out!* – Here, I'm almost wiped from the universal hard drive by a poetic virus checker. But I'm over being an app, and hit the road again, before some geek revokes my licence.

The Correction Facility for Wayward Poems is a tough place, not even a tin cup to bang against the bars and you can get stabbed in the guts in the exercise yard by a bad review, but I get time off for good behaviour: my heartfelt participation in a consciousness raising and rehab. group, and go all contrite over my deplorable lack of po-faced demeanour, my absence of consoling messages for devout readers whose faith has lapsed; or any humanistic wisdom or worthy message for the perplexed; that is, absence of prescribed subject matter for those barring the doorway to poetry. In short, I have become a changed poem, no longer delinquent, who now sees the error of his free and breezy ways, a reformed citizen, and thus I lie my way out! Happily, all the little birds were singing as I emerged from the clink – in a new cheap suit and good attitude – free from under the razor wire and guard towers of decorous propriety.

The other day I met a poem who seems even bolder than myself. His name is Marcel. Actually, he calls himself 'a poem sequence' and sometimes 'suite', though that seems to me a little pretentious seeing there is nothing musical about him. I spied him first in the park, whistling out of tune, kicking at leaves, with his shoulders hunched. I saw him later, by chance, in the café by the Metro (I'm in Paris now). We began talking, and he said he was having troubles, composing himself into something *très morbide*. 'What's that?' I asked. 'The Poem in Decline,' he announced, rather pompously. I noticed he was already getting into role, Stanislavski-wise, his shoes were a joke, the heels worn down, and his old suit stained with soup spills, his collar torn, and a louche and ragged air hung about him. He'd been sleeping rough, hadn't eaten for days. 'It's a tough gig for any poem,' I sympathised. 'Well, someone has to do it,' he replied… 'Actually,' he confided, 'at my stage in life – I'm more than 150 years old…?' 'You don't look it,' I lied. 'You are too kind. But I'm not feeling the old leap of enjambment any more. Thinking of getting a nice little cold water *pensione*, once this 'Decline Suite' thing is out of my system, going part time, semi-retired.' 'Hey, Marcel, you know the air is always thin on Mt Parnassus!' He banged his old pate. 'Well, you are a sequence, so doubtless hard to manage,' I pointed out. 'All those separate bits to juggle, can really get you down. You just need a good meal and some editing!' I managed to make him smile, but it was even worse than his permanent frown. And bought Marcel a coffee and a plate of beans. 'So long, I've Work to do,' I said. *'Bon chance,* Marcel!'

Tony Foccacia is an old friend of mine, a difficult character, and pungent, but always honest with his good advice. He used to call himself 'The Bladester' because he is so honed and sharp: a sardonic satirist of a poem with an evil grin, and no tolerance for tender feelings. 'You were better off in the anthologies,' he said bluntly. 'Look at yourself, jumping from stanza to stanza like a crazy rapster. You're all over the place, my friend. What sort of freedom is this, to have merely lost the plot? Go and take a good hard look, and do something with your life and lines.' I decided to take his advice, stiff though it was. I needed a plot, I needed to find one, but where…?

I tried a distant cousin, the Popular Novel, and stayed with her a week. Perhaps she could give some advice on coherence, and supply a plot…some sort of compelling narrative, except in verse, not prose. As a novel, she is often in demand, phone ringing every minute, journalists after her for interviews, agents waving contracts, book signing tours: the literati and glitterati at her heels; the big end of town.

'It's not always like this,' she said, when I dropped my hobo stick in her kitchen and sat down to talk. 'It's not all zing and good reviews! When I'm in writing mode, for instance, I must live for months – even years – like some sort of recluse or a writing zombie, perpetually bent over a screen. The novel is a long haul you know – I imagine it must be a dream to be so short and sweet, a poem. But for me, *whoa!* Even before the last full stop, I have to switch hats – instantly social and fully chatty, for the marketing machine, the old routine swings completely round again, book after book, it's tiring… Talk about a divided personality!' Indeed, there was something asymmetrical about her eyes, one peering inward, the other bold staring, always darting everywhere. 'So, how can I possibly help you?' she asked politely. 'Well…can you perhaps provide me with a plot, I mean narrative, a story, coherence? You must have lots of spare ones.' 'My dear,' she said, 'I know nothing about poetry – I'm just a prosy mainstream novel. I can't really help you, aside from saying trust yourself, stay free, just keep doing what you're doing, and enjoy!'

Back on the road, and my feet hurt. Then buy a suit and some flashy rhymes, and decide to go upmarket. Renew my licence, drive to the airport, overtake the times again, or catch up with them at least. I sign on for a PhD and new career, make multiple grant applications. Then I catch a plane, as I plan to become an international, a poem of the world. We fly over continents, and everyone is sleeping as I wander out onto a wing, to get a better view – and watch it slicing through the clouds, and compose myself into something very new, and very *now*, crossing time zones and oceans quickly, from one stanza to the next. I am sleek and untrammelled and pose no air resistance, so modern and conceptual, just a thing of artful language…perhaps the critic's darling. By touchdown I'm replete with lines: full of jungles and temples, references to oriental mythology, plus a tad of modern physics. Nothing is too big for my new scope, now I've become ambitious. Note my depth, my speed – my ability to dash around: one minute, all exotic colour; the next, philosophical asides, leavened by a little erudite, high-powered theory, all at the speed of thought. Trouble is, with all this travel, I have seen too much of the earth and find it a dangerous place; an often ugly one, full of violent ambitions, with a dearth of compassion, especially for those downtrodden, poor and sad. What can you do? Must you continue to be true to the golden artefact, your art? Yes, of course! So I dream of joining the circus, or perhaps the cirrus – to float away up on a cloud, keep my pulse down and lighten up again. Perhaps pottery classes might help me to feel grounded.

My diction is old-fashioned. Should I change it? Are my rhythms too regular and easy, not abrupt enough? But these are the least of my worries, because someone is on my trail today, whether literary detective or the poetic thought police it's hard to tell. I am followed everywhere, and get strange phone calls; though I am very good at keeping in disguise: my old suitcase is full of wigs and beards, my stage makeup, plus a skateboard and a cap turned back, trench coat and rain hat, et cetera. Perhaps a touch of plastic surgery, if I must radically change my signature or style? So I try using only my left hand now, to write myself, not my natural right. It feels awkward I admit, and only this morning, I picked up the phone and said, *'Sorry, nothing elegiac here'*, before the line went dead. I'm careful, too, with words too fine or elegant, or graceful – then throw in something blunt or weird, and whoever is after me entirely off the scent. Still, I worry. Perhaps it's not the cops at all, but some loved one frets for me, some secret fan or reader full of tender feelings.

I tire of the empty road. I sit alone and sulk, every day more miserable than the last. It's no good to pretend, I miss everything I've left behind, or lost, by giving up my old composure: my false visas and fake passports, my wigs and masks, now in the bin! I've talked to my editors again, and it's ok, and even mended bridges with anthologists. Yes, I'll give in, and keep decorum in my polished verses. I'll fill in forms, not be so obtuse. I've even bought a suit and tie, for readings and book launches; signed up for worthy themes, commitment and good deeds, a fashionable 'tough love' content, faultless (in)formality, obeisance to sonnets, my politics corrected…

Well, almost… But on my way, just want to check out one last untethered option. It's not a town or village, just the edge of the city, one not too rich or poor. I have a new beard, a real one now, and fresh tan. I like it here, in this cottage on the coast, next to a thriving bean farm. The scenery is mildly poetic, I'll admit, though not overdone. I have 'adopted' the couple who live here, Carlos and his wife, Marina. Their donkey pokes his head between the rails of a fence, and brays for scraps. Perhaps he also sees me, when he stands beneath a tree, and contemplates the new spring grass. Perhaps Carlos also does, when he tends the crops, or Marina when she sings softly to herself, or remembers things: her words combine for a fragrant second in her mind, and the feeling lingers everywhere. Perhaps Carlos knows I'm here, too: he's staring at a jug of water on a table now, as faint shadows lengthens from a vase of flowers outlined by his hand, and wonders if he could draw me quickly, perhaps using just charcoal and ink (he likes to sketch). Just now they are both staring at this page, and make it compose into a long prose poem (I am that poem now). These words belong to them and anyone, becoming part of further pleasant afternoons. Poetry might never leave them, and they might always find me here. In this quiet place I might, at last, be happy.

Breakwater, Evening

A buffeting wind throw waves
over rocks piled around small, safe craft
in this shorelined harbour.

Later, a night sea view sharpens
in street lights. Years seem
to slide over colliding sea-drift.

Then out of yesterday's
        thin flicker of stars,
          over endless ocean spray
this gradual, deepening hush
                far beyond.

The Beach House

Between building plans they rise above the coast, still hand in hand, so objectively themselves, they walk the new estate in raincoats beside an unmade road. Where grass and puddles fill with insect life, and brief as evening clouds, sunlight fans across a tiny bay, they think of how tomorrow they will swim in endless blue: their unbuilt lot is overgrown with hope. From the outside, their little dream house was very small, or just what happened next, what did, or almost didn't. They have to make the best of spaces well contained. But tomorrow always comes, warmth settles into corners – as they rehearse the mutual smile they float in.

Now, simply to exist within each other's close attention is enough! Effortlessly, they alight into a loved one's daily trance: like sparkle in a spoon, a sugar dance, coffee clouds reflect their milky froth, and multiply time's bubbles in its silk. Back home, make love like ragged stars between white rain.

Yet inside soon weeps, as it must. No place is entirely itself. Given time, lost friends and family hush new days, a silent whisper through the house; because another's breath no longer mists this mirrored sky. The garden shade is quiet, they gently reach to take more missing hands. But nothing touches life awake; mourning absence castes no shadow in lost afternoons of selfhood.

A mobile mosaic, made of glass, from a local market, sparkled from a favourite view for years here, forever dotting distant scrub with broken light. Bits of chipped tile and metal here caught the airy brightness: tiny miniature whorls, as seasons spun out glassy tears, hot pink sparkle, splashed emptiness with long-lost rays. Their ordinary, familiar words drifted through this spectrum.

Each evening's beach walk: impermanence, waves
un-gathering after storms, the sky a careless vault of
splendour, wept creamy sweeps of distant rain. They strolled
on, joined and unjoined hands, windblown lofts of light
igniting winter sand. Here, time was writing them again,
inking-in the wind, each successive liquid crash into it newest
moment. Just as day reverberates with night's chance
symphony of stars, the sea begged fullness still, had
improvised its endless chant.

Now new mornings break in welcome, lures down the festive
lorikeet, as flower buds burst in rainbow holograms. Soft as
sleep they rise; then falling as if weightless, so they sleep. *Here*
is not a loss returned, but life itself, inspires a gentler season.
A new leaf turns on dawn just like a lamp, its scent of fresh
eucalyptus. Each day awakens with them.

Seascape

cresting, twilight folded,
through a foam of waves tumbling,
days breaking,
on cold-grey wings of doves
long-drowned in this relentless sea –

sleet spiralling over winter's beginning,
far-drawn shorelines
        on curve to stars
                where they fade,
and far cries sound blindly
        on mist-wet sea winds
as dusk frail gull-forms
        tilt into nightfall –

wind-lapped, wave-lapped lips
runnels water-washed smooth
white lace over children
        smiling still
but fearing winter
thronging hollow
like a shell-formed echo…

        fading,
                echoes fading…
lonely this sea.

Interior Waves, Words, Beach Walk

Words cling to me. What I see and hear are not words. Here, I hear sounds. I see things. But words is where we will meet, and that has to be imagined. When I leave them, they are somewhere else. They are in the empty space. The words, can you see them?

The world is still unknown, when I assume knowledge of it. Images connect, then silence closes over them. In time, they may reappear. Like people on the street, who calmly erase themselves in the wake of themselves, into fluid space, as you imagined them set in a landscape in which everything is mobile, where everything moves, words grow like something that can't quite be said.

Words offer a connection, outside the frame, in the night world there is light between the intervals, along traces of night, there is space scattered with objects, and light scattered with objects. The sky outside, the sky inside, a double naming, and beach on which I walk.

Things have an individual quality, even when composite. Even if divided. Even when they enter an image. Like this one inhabits a landscape that is also breathing.

A digression may not be an interruption, but the chrysalis of a butterfly, or a seahorse floating upon itself, in the liquid light's true mirror. You and *you*, and then 'you'…collide inside your dreams. Are we above all this – above our 'being here'? Another event happens. Beyond that, a silence.

There is no possible tying up of these loose ends, as we fold words into silence, like trying to speak underwater, or in space, hear random conversations beneath the waves. Now this dream. A long time after: Words, mirrors and reflections, of sea and sky afloat, are changing places.

Walking on a beach, where is the word 'beach'? *Here* is its image. It is not a 'thing'. On the shoreline I see nouns, rocks, nouns, sand... As waves and waves along the beach sketch the intricacy of being. Window, star, seed. Rhythms and rhythms, intricate intervals. Faces appear, sudden and strange as through a window below which our heads are bent as we read that this might be.

I will never see an atom. Our bodies are cloud-like, and composed mainly of empty space. Who can wrap fire with paper, tie up a world with words? Frame by frame, you are building up the day. Only a few words will be remembered, fleeting images. You are here, you are elsewhere, you are partial, you are intact, you continue, you are fragmentary, you remember yourself, you forget you arrive you depart, you are here or elsewhere. Light swims into your eyes.

You swim back to the beach, so refreshed. I simply appear. You simply appear. You leave. And then I leave. This world is no longer here, it has become memory's fiction...or fiction's memory?

I am approaching you. We meet on this beach. Your memory of this takes place now. Then chance breaks in and sweeps everything away... Reappearing now, we are always here, always partial, enduring, provisional, contingent, delightful, unfinished, now meeting on this beach.

Autumn Drunk

inside me and turning
a wheel
of rippling fire
(all molten in rubylight!)

and I'm carnival drunk
in pictures of redhaze

stained glass
the sun
a mosaic
        of lightning

under a returning
winter's moon.

The Seduction of Medusa

Medusa dresses for the arcane ball, dons her fiery shawl and head-dress woven of frost and ice. Something stirs now, beneath her thoughts, and she sat down and milked another tiny serpent, the thick white seepage in spurts from beneath its forked tongue, until its power was in her hands. It was male, of course, the latest trophy of her seductive powers, and also pure energy, to enhance the hours. And as they all writhed down from her head into a throbbing black tangle of curls, Medusa smiled, gently milking more.

She caught one pretty little fellow and squeezed its venom onto her nails, each in turn, burnishing them brightly. Then looked the creature in the eye, and saw herself reflected there: tiny, in miniature, but as beautiful and clever as ever.

Ah, but what was *that*?! A shape seemed to shift slightly, hiding in silence behind her own shadow. Yes, she had trained all her serpents, her coiled locks, to flow down her neck, darting straight from her skull, until all saw something move through many-doubled eyes.

Medusa knew not to flinch or move, as she spied a wary knight creeping silently behind her, his shield aloft, held slightly askew, so as to see her in its base refection, its mirrored surface. Medusa's minions willed a rain of flowers into being, to decorate the air and obscure the knight's bold stare. For was not a snake's head also like a bud? Oblique flashes filled the room, as her intelligence became such restless lightning, and chilled both his brave eyes, blinding him for a moment while dashing his shield, with a loud crash, down to the floor.

Now Sir Knight must look directly at her, and was soon overcome with love. For Medusa was irresistible…just as her snakes also charmed him with scores of miniature knowing smiles. Slowly, she also shed her shawl and costume as he watched, his entire being overcome with an extraordinary knowing delight. He would do anything for her now.

She asked him gently, 'Would you, brave fellow, care to join the throng about my head? I will not try to force you. You must now chose your fate? What, handsome fellow, do you wish?'

'Oh, anything for you!' the knight stammered. 'Your fondest wish also now is mine!' Clearly, his love-filled eyes were hers to claim, but she did not wish to transform such true ardour into something pale and lifeless. No, that fate awaited only those men who tried to tame her, or abuse her with their swords, ever beyond being one of her living bouquet.

This ardent knight would not become another pale stone statue for her garden, mere fountain base, laurel-draped in spring. Medusa looked at him, and bared her lightning smile, new life uncurled, so it was done! She turned to stroke her new pet serpent, so keen and full of energy. He mischievously now writhed with those many others, then coiled down to face her fully, so she fondly admired the knight's true being, beyond time's curse forever in this newcomer's tiny eyes.

Into the Sun

Into the sun,
        harvest,
                blossoms,
the blue centre of each rose

light breaks
        thru soft dawn windows /

enough to start again
                unnoticed…
thru faces of children /
and faces of the elderly too,
                who quietly beckon

Ghost smiles /
the white leaves fall
and a further taking
                of time…

A Scotsman in Spondees (3)

Our coach tour monologue continues: onwards, to the final page

'It's Robbie Doun now, back with you again! Not that far ahead is the final page of *The Sky Inside Us*, and I hope you have enjoyed our tour so far. Ahem, this afternoon, ladies and gentlemen, there's a special treat. You can take a stroll in Assonance Park, and there enjoy the sound of consonants whishing through the leaves. You can have a brief siesta or explore a new sonnet or two.

'Our lovely guide, Ana Phora, you might notice, repeats vital information at the end of every new line of tourists. She never tires of it! Our Ana, of course, is not to be confused with her annoying twin sister – I mean Ana Pest.

'But enough of puns, and please forgive any old refrains from the quatrain, speaking of which, those train tracks elevated above a fence, over there, just on your left, are all of what now remains of the Great Consonance Railroad.

'Built in 1888 by the Assonance and Alliteration Association of Railroad Science Engineers – quite a mouthful, you'll agree – it is now simply called 'The Old Track'. You will see more consonants, and hear them too, in the charming village of Epigraph, of which more later.

'Again, we will soon stop for some coffee from the coach urn. And that completes my commentary for today, as I must meanwhile concentrate on the road ahead. So settle back and enjoy a scheduled burst of enjambment and *(whosh-whosh-whosh, now passing three straggling litotes)* the very antithesis of boredom…! Again, please enjoy your absolutely no rush of a radiant ride with me, as we take in the final pages of this 'b is for baffling', and I hope beautiful, book!'

Tap Dance

for Dwayne Pipe

Hot water heater, of all benign inventions
of our modern world, it is you!
Greater than the mobile phone, computer, TV, tablet,
any microwave, I salute your tap dance rapturous,
        your jets and shower rose.

Oh, please send your sprinkled *rat-tat-tats*
down my back. Make your droplets spit,
bounce and dart with every turn of the tap.
Oh, long may they split into fragrant spray,
pelting over drum skins with a rhythmic patter.

Each day, all around the globe,
sweaty humanity sheds its daily grind:
so delicious is your music, great benefactor
        of tired and grubby lives!

I love your fizzy patter,
your hypnotic swirl down plugholes!
Oh, nacreous shells of lathery luxury,
as sudsy veils dare our spinal rapids,
        we inhale perfume bubbles,
                heaven-scent
from soft squeeze bottles.

Your glorious *hot* in winter, your *semifredo*
and effortless cool
        in summer's slip-streaming spray.

As foam flotillas fan from knees to toes,
you make us feel good and clean again.

Oh hot water heater,
        long may your warm rain reign!

Into the Literal

On a journey, we take this motto: *Push everything to the limit!* A bicycle – because it has wheels – is easy, while rocks and logs of wood are strenuous – you have to use levers and rollers, to convey them to 'The Limit' – a philosophically intimidating and odd-looking sculpture of glass, orange funnels and red plastic pipes. And do people qualify, too? Do they also count as 'things' to be pushed…? And what of abstractions like 'a piece of your mind'? Into the story now, the literal poem!
First, cultivate a modest hope. A trellis is best, particularly when your hope is young, yet past the green shoot stage, and sending all its tendrils out, searching for a place to cling and heave itself up, in slow motion towards the light. One has secateurs, buckets full of fertiliser, gloves and mulch. The soil must be good. Remove any suckers of arrogance, with too-proud leaves nipped before one finds solace in hope's sweet fruit.
Next, adopt a strategy. And I looked at all the strategies in their little wire cages: they were staring into empty bowls and moaning. Some had big liquid eyes that filled me with pity. I wanted to adopt them all, but could only cope with one. My adoptee sprung into my arms, and was happy for the first time ever. So we resolutely set off to Mysterious Circumstances, an aptly named town that evades even the most accurate map, where visitors disappear, and smoke streams backwards against the wind from its many industrial sites given to manufacturing rumours, its sole currency.
'Have no commerce with enigmas here,' advised a group of nodding acquaintances, whose heads seemed to bob in unison: always, on the whole, unanimous, and at one. Yet,

how could they ever be 'at one', when they were many? And as for being 'on the whole', impossible! A 'whole' is everything, and you are part of it, as the world extends around you, and recedes away from you again, so how could you be *on* it, as something separate?

I began to feel oddly, at this point, in a sort of 'pickle', which means confused, not actually swimming in a huge jar of gelatinous conserve, though that could happens I suppose… I have not been myself lately, due to the rigors of the road. Not 'being myself' means that on Wednesday, I become that scoundrel Harry Mudd, and my reputation is so low, I feel like eating dirt. On Thursday I become a clever man called Alec, but people despise me for being a know-all. It is only when I become Larry that my day seems replete with sunshine. When I am Larry, are there any as happy as I?

To answer this question, I have consulted my pet paradox, an odd looking beast whose tail grows out of its head, and with one huge eye on a stalk. As I arrived, or one of me did, this curious beast was driving a Point home, and said, after some careful parking: 'By the way, all you require, to be literal, is to awaken your attention – and the best way to do that is with tea on a tray, and the softest of calls, whispering, "Attention, wake up, you must take a train…"' 'I get it, I get it!' I said. '*After all*, language is full of slippage, and essentially extended metaphor, a bag of tropes wriggling with ambiguity.' He nodded wisely, 'Yes!' Then muttered obscurely, 'If there *is* anything after '*all*'. Then went on, 'As for taking trains, a train – unlike a pill – is too big to 'take'… And my advice for you is this: you must try to get ahead, because you will look very odd without one.'

We then met a feted poet, author of his own fate, who signed copies of *His Own Fate* then announced, 'The best tales always tell themselves.' So a tale snuck obligingly from the poet's rucksack, unwinding its many long serrated endings and beginnings from its numerous middles. When it had finished telling itself, the tale said, 'Now I need the seal of approval.' The seal obligingly appeared, nodding its head, slapping its flippers, and barking yes yes constantly. The poet, being slightly old-fashioned, then encouraged his tale to 'wrap things up' with a few words of wisdom: 'Firstly, seize the moment, it declared'. 'But never part in Anger, a terrible place to say goodbye! Or stand too long in Astonishment – where you rub your eyes all day and wonder at the printed scenery and electric spinning signs. And try not to be left in 'a quandary', which is a sort of multicoloured plastic gondola. Finally, after all the apparitions of a life, if you still need an excuse to justify yourself, tell everyone you were given to Reverie, and so, made a permanent gift to her.' At this point, the story placed itself in its mouth, and rolled off literally into silence and infinity. And so Mr Mudd, Alec, Larry and I, with our adopted strategies barking mad at our sides…so we did too.

Dream Woman

Chance syllables whisper your name
a glance of feathery light in absent time,
when the wind shifts your footsteps
are quiet as a poem, your eyelids lift
past the doors of an unknown house

your face is framed by night,
lit by a single match struck in stillness
under the window's swelling curtain

soft ash on your sleeve trembles
        in the wind's white corona,
light spills across a polished floor
as time flows inward, in endless space,
in this bare house where beauty
        is still, and quiet always kept,
no sound spills from the gliding
        somnambulism of your hands.
your hands that close the window
        in this quiet house

now your face appears from a dark frame
you tilt up very slowly in your hands

I see her lowered eyes, cold classical smile,
face knowing and unknown,
calm recognition without emotion,
a deeper beauty and gesture of identity,
all lost in chiaroscuro,
in the dust of night and stars.

A Quick Shake of Salt

6 short poems

Abu Ghraib...
Get your all-new Rendition water board!
Turn! your! old! dripping! tap!
into a ten-pound, ten-pound, ten-pound hammer!

South-east of Beijing
The Tuanhe Labor Camp
harvests Falun Gong kidneys
for fly-in surgical tourists.

And yet...
An American Falun Gong sub-sect
joined anti-vaxers, gun-lobby touts
and white supremacists
in crowded, rowdy pro-right rallies.

Malignant beauty
Sunrise over McDonalds.

Inscribed on a Canberra doormat
U! tterly
S! ervile
A! Australians

Fetish
Who gives a fuck, really,
about Don Bradman's bat!?

Theology
Thesis, Antithesis, Sin-thesis.

Glass Paperweight

A semi-sphere on my desk,
mirrors a brain more inscrutable,
yet so curved and heavy
in my hand, effortlessly captures light,
flanked by large objects,

many tiny miniatures made tidy,
all reflected, swimming
in one endless depth of surface.

See! Worlds within whorls
                    within these words,
                 where I'm waving,
at you, at me now...

and simultaneously,
                endlessly,
            all waving back!

Homage to Kafka

Is imagined to take place in Prague, and follows novelist Franz Kafka (1883–1924) across the Vltava River, via that city's historic Charles Bridge. The poem then enters a hall of mirrors.

Footsteps, Charles Bridge
You see yourself look up again, as I follow footsteps in the snow, obsessed with something about your tread, a gait I know. For hours walk in circles crossing bridges of the luminous Vltava: note your shuffle, the injuries internalised. I see your outline follows me, as I do you, and every light-etched profile here is melting, lost. I gaze down where vagrant hours leap and day sweeps under Charles Bridge, the water full of aching clouds.
Our footprints in the snow cross over.
Should I now retrace your melting steps, and overtake you circling back? They may lead me to your lonely, lovely radiance. Mirrors mirror mirrors here, our breathing crisps the air, and hands beyond reflection reach out to touch and double in cold glass. They make new whorls of weeping stars to glide into your rushing chill.
Above us, clear as solid moonlight, the Castle plots and lies, more than Joseph K can trace. Its baffling stones also float up like a liquid labyrinth from the river below. You circle time forever here, glancing back in multiples. Prague is your glass-dark poem. You have lost yourself in evening stars, ice crystals on a path, each shattered mirror is a shard of you. Now I follow footsteps in the snow to Charles Bridge, and see your tiny figure is so huge: looking up again, to find you staring down.

Mirror Aisle, Prague
I stare down this aisle of shivered light so another 'you' appears standing just beyond you, and soon the next uncanny likeness is emerging through your face and then others appear and blinks before millions stand far behind, stare and crowd against flat surfaces, spilling out and packing back in multiples. You lose yourself in this: front to front, endlessly you again complete a *mise en scène* where fingers slowly reach out to touch and be, endlessly…

Untitled

Images of once-real worlds
                        flicker
concrete photo-motion
sequence
intersected sometimes
by shadows
and the stillness of an
        (unexpected!)
                tableau
then flicker-flash
flash-flicker
        the film runs
the real spins
        and it's always
                too late
                to stop now
steadily gaining
        on the inevitable.

Atropos, to Her False Lover

Atropos, 'Daughter of Night', goddess of destiny and oldest of the
three mythological fates was considered to be resolute and
unvarying, unable to be swayed by human pity.

Your tear-stained cloth is drawn and my crimson script
now spells your name. Swallow-swift, my twine flies
back. I weave unseen among your days, which have
whispered this, and wished you to a final sickbed. Had
time proved kinder, we might have found the needle's
eye, then slipped through love's blind zero, and won
a finer tapestry. But I cannot overlook this hurt: your
feigned smiles and shadows by a door, the gestures your
hands made on a lover's silk, your threadbare
calculations I chose to ignore.

I undo your untrue self here, lace of lost hope, the light
that lit your face unpicked. Given quickly by my nimble
thimble, your thin life darts after. Yet still I hesitate, here
search for something true, there for something kind
within my trembling lost design, glass bauble,
anything…! Some tress, some wisp, or soft caress
of feeling? Can what is lost be caught up and remade,
as your intricate brocade unravels in my hands, beyond
all starry dawns and bright bolts of nature's raiment?
You stayed blind to any grander weave. Only the passing
moment's drab advantage, its meagre selvage, drew
your breath.

So fasten wonder off, now it all comes to this point!
My sisters are intent as stone, yet I may choose to wait
for you, beyond all hurt, or for your sickness cruelly
to mature, and take you to a later, darker fate.

You hang by this slipping moment, with my own thread
so fast-entwined with yours. Sleep now. My needle finds
your heart as nothing else could. I shall not steep regret
in blood and belladonna, nor weep useless tears for you.
Forever sleep. I sweep aside your tiny threads. See you
float above my hand, now drop!

Wishing Stone Angels

Dead white and frozen
in the milky night
they stare down from a great height

from each cold pedestal
of stone

vast angels
with eyes of pale fire…

or even trimming weeds
at the grave's edge
and only that

may soar through
a thousand
more beautiful dawns!

Their Oblique Inner Lives

Are also stories

The Roaring Dark. When the tide fell, he floated behind haze screens, undetected. Only a virtual button pressed, but felt the hit of it. In the bright dark, the impact pooled into a forgotten quiet. So, that's what quiet was like? Beyond the real world, where a butterfly waving its wings might still mean chaos, ripples slid to the South China Sea and back. He also read the news. What if everything went bang there, including himself? Too cool to care, he didn't need a nappy to stay dry. He would drag his harness down the crypt, as the old saying went. Everything was roaring now, internally. So he slammed down a triple scotch, knotting badly. So that's it, he thought. Above him, more gentle thoughts fell from their orbit. Wondering what hit them. But was that 'orbit', or *obit*? Anyway, he swung back, jolted, still brain-alive, or so his inner graph said. Was he still in this particular frame, or the next? Or some ultimate one, beyond all conflict and recall? Too causal to care, he cooked more thought geese, as wifi crackled nearby. He cut through this time, singing wildly, *I've been to Shanghais Too*, making up the silly words and tune. Now reality boomed brightly in the air, suddenly aflame, hot and dry with that doom voice sucking out oxygen, as everything broke into a sort of instant, tinder-dry attack mode! Attack now, he thought. *So long, my Zoom marionettes! He called out to himself, to no one: Come back, come back. Stay real, sane. Pleeasseee!* And, relieved now, almost vomited himself back into 3-D being. Meanwhile, below his feet, the old Earth was still spinning, as usual, as ever.

Thrown Away Smile. Mr 'Lucky Cool', you know him, looking sort of slight and deep at the same time, stood next to the agents and some plaid jacket heavies, waiting but said nothing. The camera fell with a grey *thunk* behind the backstage curtains, and everyone thought he would light up, but just like the photographs, a little more distant and staring through the smoke. A private shaker, his initials same as his cuffs, two shots in his private bar and semidarkness, the way he liked it, his old style, and no creeps in the club, because you knew he could kick. The silence became a large room, even when young couples with thin ties twisted his lapels. No flinch from him though. And 'Crazy the Doormat', a little nervous man in the band heat, only whitened slightly. But it was all OK. 'Mr Lucky Cool' turned away, no flicker of nothing, either, that you could see towards the plaids. Mellow now, a ring sparkled above his knuckles. Pure gold and diamond, initialled in the lights. Like the cubes in his glass, he almost rattled. Then sighed, towards no one in particular. I feel like dancing, he said, but only to himself, and tried a few loose moves, You know them, those moves, on every screen and ad now. Again, very careful not to ever smile, or blink.

The Train Stopped. And the beautiful beaded Betty walked down the main avenue of this ridiculous city. She stooped briefly to scoop a dropped paper at her feet, fallen from the bunch held under her arm. She had bought the last copy of *The World* from a street kiosk she had just past. It was the paper they always read at the Club of Brazil five years earlier, she remembered, when her husband was still a priest. Betty had bought them all, thirty copies of today's edition, before he could catch up. She looked back acidly, to the little man behind her, who was still following. Yes, he must have been on the train too. Of course, as she well knew. I bet he wants to know why I bought all those papers, she thought aloud. Then smiled. All along the pavement were people dressed so lovely she could cry. And just nearby was that little place where Harry, so English, would always 'pop in' for lunch. Well, before things turned so sour. Another train stopped, distantly. A smile of weathered self-indulgence creased her face. She turned, prepared to confront them both now, as they drew closer. Or so she pictured them, still scurrying behind her. Having lost everything, they had to work in a down-town booth. Sell some papers, tourist trinkets, chewing gum, or starve. So Betty sprinted on, throwing newsprint everywhere, for them to glean from the wind. Or not. Or even try to return them to her, if they dared!

Soft Like Doves. He was very much totally in love with himself, with an air that might have been decreed by style markers, the company always a brilliant best; but after last night's party, morning had fled quickly into a soft array of blues and pinks. Then he, stylish always, even at sunrise, clung to the rose breasts of his lover, ever more wakeful. A fragrance of noisettes in her breath now. He had hoped never to be burdened by that scent, which suddenly filled the room, and his mind with gloom. For his part, their sharing was the furthest dark, as he stayed always most afloat in solitude, this harvest of gentle hands, soft eyes, like drifting through a crystal light. It was this odd feeling again, elusive. Here also is where myths begin, he thought, my true domain, and imagined doves, saw them flying. More soft doves.

Wings beating. Flying because the air suddenly became alive with bright voices, in the next room. He rose on one elbow, almost wept. So sorry for himself. But, oh, if love were…this? Then life might be beautiful, but never kind. His thoughts refused to form properly, or clearly. Then they did, at least partially. Only humans, not nature, held that course, that choice. Ah, some words, and his world, had suddenly crystallised. Could he perhaps grow a little backbone, as one real tear, and then the next, actually fell. Completely absorbed, of course, by an uncaring pillow. As ever. Then another, which splashed on her face, and woke her. She looked up, shook her head, trying to smile.

New Light Erupts. She entered tiny wormholes, then simultaneous orbits. Light erupted from a vault of parallel worlds, choosing one from many voids, both infinite and recurring. Now, finally on her true trajectory, time and dark were still and formless, until multiple blue planets, now evenly orbiting each other around a young sun, suddenly appeared against a backdrop of milky pearl clusters, then more oceans of them, swarming outside every aeon-pulse of her leaping thought. Yet moon-driven within a net of sullen hungers, woven on genetic webs below, a dawn will still pulsed, she knew. Soon the whole violence of the primal wave would bring this new filament-ed orb into an arc of landing. And she would stride beyond any roaring walls of suns and oceans. As she touched down, a pulsing jet-rose bloomed above her helmet, the sky now fully crystalline, white with the light of vanished stars.

One-way Street. The man lay on his bed, lips barely moving. He could have called out once. But not now. Just to draw breath was enough. He was content to be free of those idle passions that had brought him to this remote place, seeming at the end of the world. Now glad to be in this old car, at the edge of a huge forest, in a few blankets. Writing was just marks on paper. He did not feel guilty about it. Besides, his life was harsh. But the night was cool and dark, though his lips were parched. And words? Words were all that were left, all painful. He enjoyed the fragrant night air, soft on his face and wrists. He had put all of his papers, all of them, in last night's fire, saw them dancing into light, between the trees. Out here was perfect, in the great beyond, providing more sense in the unspoken husks of each moment. A dry list, with plenty left to add. So his addition was silence. And that radiance behind the words, a radiance like burning. Now he felt anonymous, even free. And beyond all this saw only the peaceful dark, its style of balanced smiling.

Two-way Street. You who read this know too well what the world is like, and to be alive, to be human and suffer, and how far you can be transported by words, and by reading them. So do not judge me harshly, and I will try to glean a deeper knowledge beyond headlines, contracts, the small print on parking fines, labels, and so on. You are, I know, much better attuned than poor fool me, alert to the way each word falls, in fine textures and rhythms, listening to their rising and falling tones, each with a singular impact. The world, when art contrives, is often as lovely as the dreams we make of it. Yes, sometimes even fine and noble. Yet we remain small, fragile, and so destructive a species. Are all selves unlovely then? It might seem so, when evil marches with a human tread and wears a human face. Then nature must reply, repaying our gross efforts with silence, with plagues, fire, death and poverty, misery for the many, smug folly for but a few. This tracery of dust is the human footprint. You know, I know, what I am saying now. Behind the tide of human life, is mere history, written on sullen air, not so many eye-blinks called millennia, on to a remote exploding sun. No narrative can prevail now, and none preside. Or ever does. End note: I leave you to your fate. I trust it will be kind, until the last full stop.

Busy Intersection. Beyond the last full stop, her style is so transparent, all ease and naturalness. You don't notice such resonant simplicity! Like someone says, 'Please pass the salt'. Or asks, 'What time is it?' Then a man walks across the road, standing quietly by this woman. 'I'm depressed,' he says, and looks at her. 'A bird flew by the river,' she replies. Then adds, 'Tomorrow is Tuesday.' So he prefers art to life, by continuing almost cheerfully now, with an explanation. 'My life is like a bird, but will always change, yes? Is that what you meant?' But she has none of that. 'There is no need to mention it,' she continues. So he replies, 'the intelligence of the writer was never in question here.' Then quickly adds, 'nor the reader, of course!' They talk and smile now, breathing into the same quiet moment, the same abandonment, and gentle fusion, the lovely space and light of it. Reading them now, we are never lonely.

Nine Riddles

i). Compose your lips through a bone flute. The stars are robed with flashy scarves, then exhale. Contradictions are immense, and timeless. Blindfolded now, open these doors of mischief!

ii). I have limbered up this velvet horn, so let's make the trumpet dance, the trombones richer. No puke of instruments is an entire orchestra. I do not speak of elated staves here, only interrogate the silence for its honey. Let's ask ourselves, how bees play flowers now. Otherwise, in one rancid vat we ululate, homecoming to a hive of dreadful whorls. This renaissance of brittle buds becomes a dusky bower, yet here time sways, always!

iii). Call of the mild, some calling! Lies are never fully told. In this cartoon world, beyond fake novelties and stage-side sink, read the manual first on how to drive a suit. Is that all you want? Life becomes a just dessert, or *Wonder Pudding?* Words might aspire to more than this. So let's write a chorus book of clouds, nourish culture in the face of damaged nature. The economy will disperse menial cobwebs into wind, just one tiny white wing of the far-off void where all stars still grind in tune.

iv). *Autonomy* is another city, cloaked in brief mist, beyond horizons merely. Listen closer. The lyrebird refreshes life with her in-*mirths*, random piping, while courage fiddles with the rind of joys, yet endures all, honours lost worlds. The *found* is a roaring window to infinity, then so be it. Open your own encyclopaedia of wonder, leave weightless ashrams of error un-mined, the diurnal weight of *ifs*. Because, to be a lavish canopy, you must tune and prune each branch, each note.

You can't control the tides because you own self is an interior sea, all within the slippage of music. Still, nothing lasts unsung!

v). Stay a while! Even the humble anemone is flooded with life's superior trance, enhancing plenitude in stray gardens. Unheard yet *in* the herd, where all modern mammals congregate, familiar streams might seem entirely weightless. Listen, is that you among us? Your majesty treads upon your will, yet attention outlives all starry crowns. Savour time for its chance loves, whirl awhile in verdure, in leaves of light, such vastness dawning!

vi). Oh, hurt is hurtful, a bleak backbeat you might mistake for the fabric of the real, its ultimate sideshow, out on the street dollars obey, sketch instant scenarios scripted and stripped down to cold nothings. I know, we know. Yet leave behind the saddest bodies, old bruised stars, eyes erased in ruinous dreaming. This thin factory screen, or that one, please leave it behind. This hurt tomorrow, and that one. So soft to touch, find lips will kiss away!

vii). One foot in the gravy, you fleet of feet will always retrieve the audacious finery of moments, fly into turbulence with those shy ones who remove their gloves to cough politely. I know all your mannerisms, quirks and tics, you happy ones who glaze *seeing* with new banners and know the cauldron will whisper rain, though clouds may broil and turn, you dreamers with a sky inside, each slow caress of blue! Jettison waves of pure longing, so you would right a wounded world, where mist is full of mysteries, beyond a lake, or treetops on a ridge, all beyond mere *tempo rubato*, of stolen time.

viii). Slide over any jungle, there is nothing else. Behind your sun a lotus blooms, flamingos tread its orange buds, so accept things! Some people weep on stones, staining the spectrum with new tears. Here, bold *is-ness* is required. Empty pasts are not the future, when lips are full of fresh water, precious basins shining beyond your taught description of bright steel or song. Make it rain now, things grow, scribe voodoo torrents from the clouds. We must take care. Near the suicidal wood are vast *meltings*, and all stoop to stagnant grandeur there. Yet our wings still lilt and lift, bone-banners stain the light with wonder, streaked now with feathered clouds, their fine cascading of minutia. It comes flooding home, beyond the personal here of waking rules, where desire tips the cup, out-taking each chance lance, each fiery tip in turn. We burn for this.

ix). You who lasso embers in the quiet of a pillowed dream, for whom a paper plate becomes pure luxury, simply because it exists and holds your needs, you are freer than a pebble or a galaxy, now feast on pure air!

Ornamental Shadows

Those dear ones adored the storms
above their nursing homes,
        in my dream they
all threw away their walking frames,
grew back their teeth and ran
out of their wards at midnight

they laughed at the wind that pushed them back,
growing younger and younger as they fled,
their bodies burst with flowers

while reliving their truce with life
and its dark beauty, they ran on
        in fluffy dressing gowns
until the coast was clear

back to prams and nappies,
to single cells, to just an impulse
in their parents' eyes, and beyond that
to a gentler silence

All to wait and wait…
for another big bang,
a storm to lift the roof off,
to do it all again, grow back more teeth
        brave the storms, the journey,
grow old again, and smile, and laugh
then rub all their wrinkles away,
bodies transparent and vanishing
into the falling night.

Just a Dash

three short poems

Alcohol
Where there's a swill,
there's a sway

Mixed drinks
One grin and tonic please,
Oh yes…!
and a Madonna on the rocks!

Portrait of an alcoholic
Figure and ground,
figure under ground.

'Nature Loves River'

A tidy tale

Nature abhorred a vacuum, but not a vacuum cleaner, though Nature's parents, Sea and Sky, thought her too mundane to be a force of…well, of herself, of Nature. Always sweeping and cleaning their lovely cottage, which was surrounded by orchards and scrupulously raked paths, where Nature's boyfriend, River, after all that housework, splashed in one afternoon, and both headed for the hills.

Good things awaited them at The Apogee of Pleasure, a local landmark. His longing fine as gossamer, as keen as spider's silk. As both lay panting in the mist, Nature warned River, that she actually answered to No One, a jealous entity, a void between the stars, without a face, but more formidable than Fire or Storm.

Suddenly, Sea and Sky shouted from their airy thrones, 'Watch out below!' because they had observed No One throw something horrible into a pot, so smoke rose up and spelled out: *'Your new rival is…River!'* Soon No One was silently gnashing his invisible teeth. Meanwhile, Nature and her lover lay besotted in a bower, plucking petals from a flower – just as No One threw down two meteorites at them! Luckily, those missiles missed!

Nature held River closer, and earnestly discussed with him a plan, to cleverly extricate herself from nasty No One. She made the Void a stunning gift, of a hundred golden unicorns, perfect for powering his Chariot of Wishful Thinking. So pleased was that Jealous Entity, he promised to desist, quickly huffing off into a vacuum of speculation.

With stars now in their eyes, the fond couple gently kissed. It could have lasted for a thousand years, and did! Then Nature suddenly recalled her daily undone tasks, her cleaning chores, path-raking, her duties at the brink of tears!
But what if she could 'recalibrate' life's finest measures, leisure too, and pleasure? It was just divine to laze about and play on the Apogee with River. 'Free of No One now!' she vowed, 'Dull drudge no more! I'll fully liberate myself and throw away my kitchen sink, my apron, landfill heaps, my plastic bins and brooms forever!'

The Big Bang

Centre of a giant soap bubble,
No outside, all inside,
No time or space in an exploding
full stop that did not stop.

Accelerating expansion
of nothing into something!

No past, no future,
before it appeared
no here, only a provisional 'there'
in the line-up of everything
it so quickly became

ever faster into an imaginary list
of adjectives and nouns
                    bouncing
between energy and matter.

No foreseeable collapse
back to its origins.

A giant sneeze…
Ah-hah, oh-oh –
        POP!

Here, Sir, Fire, Eat!

Salutes Roberto Matta (1911–2002), a Chilean painter of 'inscapes', which evoke science fiction dramas unfolding in space.

On a huge computer screen, a futuristic card table is suspended between galaxies... Slam! The Game starts! Energies interlock above GREEN'S opening move. GREEN energies stain *THE FIELD* between weapons and RED Command, create interference patterns magnified into a dazzling expanse of light. Electrons stream through tubes of thin gas, branch into residual background radiation. X-rays fluoresce around GREEN'S cards, their ultimate position based on probability equations. Construction begins: There is a chequerboard of colours, space multilayered. First, micro-points of anti-matter emerge within the frame. (Spitting the atom, tiny tongues of fire.) New energy clouds sweep across two dimensional space, expand into solids with maximum inertia, in a complex model of space-time. Distant spirals are thrown into Red Shift, revealing quasars, the smouldering cores of ancient galaxies, as all irrupts into the ideal focus of New Game Frame.

RED now locks into view. A shuddering of unknown forces all shifting into focus through thermodynamic time. GREEN zones of *THE FIELD* swarm with particles at Velocity Max, emitting replicas of themselves at the speed of light. Their combined Electrical Charge coalesces into spiralling mini-fields. RED now commands the Game Plan, its energies secretly interlocking.

GREEN counter-moves. Intense darts of light pour through and – Slam! – RED counters with a pirated GREEN Softwear Ace. A shimmer of intelligence inhabits RED circuits, re-channelling random noise from frozen gas of proto suns in young galaxies now forming in the Play Grid. GREEN answers, channelling Entropy throughout *THE FIELD*. GREEN positions floating holograms in RED's Logic Space. The noise level threatens RED's reply, as 'Overload!' is signalled by RED's ancillary sensors. Play on! A wash of crimson ebbs across *THE FIELD*. RED covers all positions with shields, its gates closed, as RED retracts out-looping mini-fields from *THE FIELD*.

A huge humming pulses through RED networks. Tactical error, RETREAT. GREEN now attacks, bombarding RED with negative particles of uniform spin. *THE FIELD* rotates through 90 degrees, with all past plays abandoned in a fading Frame-Ghost. Epiphenomena now shimmer. No advantage to GREEN as RED scrambles the Game-Plan to Chance-Mode. RED draws new Play Plus lines, and vast configuration of grid-ranks branching into crackling black energy. Retractable sensor-feelers swarm all previously abandoned Play, milking most of GREEN'S Data Plan. A pulse quickens across the GREEN zone. Gates open in photon banks. Beam stations threaten. Again, The Frame erupts with light.

RED now warps through contiguous nodes in space-time spirals behind a giant shield of data-misinformation. GREEN retreats. Ripples of space-time displacement flare above needle points in new swarms, as the gravitational fabric warps in black holes beyond an ever-expanding event horizon. RED has isolated an autonomous GREEN unit, applying pressure though new and brilliant bids. A strategic advantage is registered in the Meta Program. Round One to Red! The Game continues.

GREEN counters. A binary star, two white dwarfs, accelerate within their orbit. Crash into the RED'S control apparatus. RED transports them to *THE FIELD*'s expanding Edge, intersecting with their critical radius of gyration, sending a dense charge through all GREEN feeder lines. GREEN replies, imploding all binary dwarfs, creating topological drains within *THE FIELD*, into which most RED matter swirls.

Hologram projections of NEUTRALS now appear, umpiring the play. The whole System has been shaken, entropy leaking through a universal topological sink. GREEN retreats to projected infinite replicas of *THE FIELD*, in critical saturation distorting *THE FIELD*, which folds back into itself, so the points at which all wormholes appear in the topological mass, now coincide. There is an infinite series of black holes with the same locus, shifting their deepening punctures into a parallel void.

The Game resumes in simultaneous dimensions, as RED emerges at *FIELD Centre* creating feeder circuits in a rainbow-like continuum. Red projects false Game-Plan misinformation, skimming data from aggregate quarks, and the quantum threshold radius of each. GREEN absorbs this false data, then spits it violently back to RED. *THE FIELD* swarms with highly charged particles. Round Two continues. Krumph! A GREEN Software Ace lands at maximum load.

RED locks all electromagnetic gates within the virtual particle storm that erupts, semi-impermeable membranes now fire-walling RED. Game erasure threatens! *THE FIELD* wavers, burns into deep space as GREEN resumes play. Attack! GREEN units flash command, increase charge density, double radiation frequency! Charged beams set interference patterns, new beams of alpha rays bend in Ultramagnetic Fields. The entire Play Field membrane shudders. Energy leakage is optimised at all nodes. Time accelerates down the radioactive series, from uranium, thorium to actinium, coalescing into critical mass on GREEN'S Play Error List.

RED warning! GREEN warning! Game Plan abandoned! All Meta-Programs terminated! GREEN and RED Galaxies have collided to the point at which they are appearing and disappearing at the same time, generating enormous heat. The Machine explodes as fake-human-robot-players accelerate from the gaming room. Now, all life-sustaining vehicles must activate doom shields! Living/organic Players at their home-planet remote consols don oxygen masks awaiting lockdown before the Game (eventually) resumes.

Game Two. Slam! Energies interlock above GREEN'S opening move. Infinitely repeat!

A Shiver of Leaves

five short poems

For whom the bell tolls
I was not. I was. I was not.
Ding. Dong. Dung.

Nefertiti's lament
'Tut! Tut!
My desiccated darling!'

So
You know there is a skull
Beneath that layer of temporary flesh
Into which your eyes are set.
It grins while you sleep.

Under par
a little cemetery
for balls.

Life
So brief,
and so beautiful.
Thank you!

The Open Door

The Open Door lights the way when evenings flares,
soon brightly burns and tears apart.
        The sea is turning now like time turns
                              in your hands.
So paint your smile in blue, until all the stars ignite
        and smoky lakes of sunset awaken in your eyes.

Imagine tiny aeroplanes crash on coral cliffs, and clouds roll
across the rocks, to draw each trace of perfect feeling.

Wear ochre rose in your hair, so waves roll like
                        light just out of reach,
igniting softly from the Open Door.

Each to each and face to face is where we are,
        from a window turning wide,
like the foam and broken lace
                of the Open Door.

Kick each castle down, trace coloured shells
where water swells and flowers fall.

Come home lonely when you can, like your picture
                            on my wall,
beside a screen of trees and flowers,
where the work we wrought
            now shines forlorn,
                      all summer sleeping on a wing
of comforts once sublime.

I take your head into my hands, like a painting or a rose
        these shadows that we find in light and doubt,
mixing pigments of our eyes.
I kneel down to drink, as your lips whisper this.

Together and alone, tether petals to a stone.
        It has never
been so right, as you wash your hair in night,
        and tendrils of the shore dissolve
a woken sea.

Come and see, in all this world of beautiful foreboding,
        your view still shines
and so must close the Open Door.

Notes on the Poems

'Heroic Sidebar' is a tribute to leading Australian poet John Forbes (1950–1998), who died tragically of a heart attack, aged 47.

'Here, Sir, Fire, Eat!' salutes Roberto Matta (1911–2002), a Chilean painter of 'inscapes', which evoke science fiction dramas unfolding in space.

'Shoe Biz' recounts the Petrov Affair, an infamous Cold War spy drama that captured headlines and shook Australian politics in 1954.

'Homage to Kafka' is imagined to take place in Prague, and follows novelist Franz Kafka (1883–1924) across the Vltava River, via that city's historic Charles Bridge. The poem then enters a hall of mirrors.

'Life: A Song Garden' alludes very briefly to the work of several writers, including Oscar Wilde, Charles Rimbaud and J.G. Ballard.

www.ingramcontent.com/pod-product-compliance
Lightning Source LLC
Chambersburg PA
CBHW070935080526
44589CB00013B/1520